Contents

Abstract

The Arctic: A New Partnership Paradigm or the Next "Cold War"?

Global climate change is impacting the global security environment, most notably in the Arctic

region. While many nations have been planning, preparing, and programming to exploit the

opportunities presented in a receding-ice Arctic, the United States has lagged far behind in all of

the substantive actions necessary to preserve its vital national interests in the region. Analysis of

the actions of the five Arctic coastal nations, sans the United States, reveal significant advances

in military presence, infrastructure expenditures, territorial claims, and political maneuvering as

these nations jockey to consolidate and preserve their perceived sovereign rights and national

interests in the region. Further analysis shows partnership is key to advancing United States'

interests as budgetary and political pressures preclude unilateral action. As a result,

recommendations center around building U.S. international legitimacy and credibility, exploiting

a critical capability gap as a uniting issue, and capitalizing on a dearth of unifying military

cooperative constructs to lead a new partnership paradigm. The United States stands at a

strategic crossroads; failure to act erodes the Nation's ability to shape the Arctic policy

environment.

Introduction

Global climate change is bringing about epochal transformation in the Arctic region, most notably through the melting of the polar ice cap. The impact of these changes, and how the global community reacts, may very well be the most important and farthest reaching body of issues humanity has yet faced in this new century. A number of nations bordering the Arctic have made broad strides toward exercising their perceived sovereign rights in the region, and all except the United States have acceded to the United Nations Convention on the Law of the Sea (UNCLOS); UNCLOS provides an international legal basis for these rights and claims.[1] Similarly, while most Arctic nations have been planning, preparing, and programming resources for many years in anticipation of the Arctic thaw, the United States has been slow to act on any of the substantive steps necessary for the exercise of sovereign rights or the preservation of vital national interests in the region.[2]

The United States must move outside the construct of unilateral action in order to preserve its sovereign rights in the Arctic, capitalize on the opportunities available, and safeguard vital national interests in the region. In today's budget-constrained environment and as a Nation at war with higher resource priorities in Iraq and Afghanistan than in the Arctic, it is unrealistic to believe that any significant allocation will be programmed for addressing this issue.[3] Since the United States is too far behind in actions necessary to preserve its vital national interests as compared to the other Arctic countries, the Nation must take the lead to cultivate a new multilateral partnership paradigm in the region.

A new partnership framework is vital to pooling the many capabilities of the Arctic nations and ultimately leveraging these capabilities for the preservation of the United States' interests. Analysis will show a dearth of unifying military partnership constructs on anything

1

other than a bilateral or trilateral basis, and reveals that search and rescue operations may be the —glue" that ultimately binds the Arctic nations' military forces together. While the opportunity for and types of partnerships are expansive, the scope of the recommendations is limited to accession to UNCLOS, sponsorship of a unifying multinational arctic exercise, and establishment of a comprehensive military partnership framework. To this end, background information illustrating the magnitude of the problem is offered followed by a brief review of differing opinions on U.S. partnership, analysis of the actions and preparedness of other Arctic nations, examination of some existing partnership frameworks and opportunities, and concluding recommendations for the U.S. theater-strategic leader in the Arctic.

Background: The United States is Unprepared

The Arctic is the fastest warming region on the planet and scientific models forecast an ice-free summer Arctic sea within 30 years with some predictions as early as 2013.[4] As the Arctic ice cap recedes, expansive virgin areas rich in natural resources and new, commercially lucrative maritime routes open for exploitation by those nations most prepared to capitalize on these opportunities. The potential for economic gain is enormous as 10 percent of the world's known and an estimated 25 percent of undiscovered hydrocarbon resources exist in the region, 84 percent of which occurs offshore.[5] Transportation of these resources pose high profit potential as well. For example, tanker traffic between northern Russia terminals and Southeast Asia ports can save $1 million in fuel costs using an Arctic routing instead of the Suez Canal.[6] Those countries with the requisite capability stand to be handsomely rewarded.

An essential resource in the Arctic is a fleet of ships capable of ice breaking operations. They are essential not only for the maintenance of waterways and ship escort when sea ice is present, but for the additional duties of year-round sovereignty projection, search and rescue,

2

resource protection, and rule of law enforcement; notably, none of the U.S. icebreakers are configured for these additional duties.[7] Two of the three U.S. Coast Guard's icebreakers, POLAR SEA and POLAR STAR have exceeded their service lives, both of which are currently nonoperational and constitute America's entire heavy ice capability.[8] POLAR SEA is undergoing repairs with an expected return-to-service date of June 2011; POLAR STAR requires extensive repairs and upgrades with an expected completion some time in 2013.[9] The third is a medium class ship configured for scientific research support and unable to handle thick Arctic ice. Cost estimates in 2008 dollars are $800 to $925 million for a new ice breaker with a 10 year lead time and $800 million to extend the lives of the two POLAR class ships.[10] The National Research Council in its 2007 report to Congress stated that —U.S. icebreaking capability is now at risk of being unable to support national interests in the north and the south."[11] In contrast, the Russians maintain a fleet more than six times and the Canadians four times larger than the United States.[12] To catch up with other Arctic nations in ice breaking capability alone, the expenditure would be at least $20 billion taking decades to complete.[13] While the icebreaker issue outlined above is but one of many aspects of the United States' inability to address vital national interests in the Arctic, it is indicative of the magnitude of the problem facing this nation. With little organic capability in the region, partnership may seem a natural solution to the United States' Arctic issues with accession to UNCLOS providing the international cooperative basis for further multilateral endeavors. However, there exist a number of differing opinions on partnership and UNCLOS.

Opposing Views of Partnership

There is significant resistance within the U.S. Congress not only against UNCLOS, but also against any multilateral partnerships. A small but influential group of conservative senators ardently block the UNCLOS treaty from ratification; this effective opposition accounts for some 16 years of "consideration" on the issue.[14] Their rationale asserts that accession to UNCLOS forfeits too much U.S. sovereignty and that existing customary international law plus a powerful navy already protects national interests.[15] Further arguments claim that UNCLOS will curtail the U.S. Navy's freedom of movement and states the historical precedence of international law preserving the peace in the Arctic need not be altered.[16] Others propose a new regulatory regime reasoning that UNCLOS founders could not have envisioned the Arctic circumstances faced today. One such proposal is a construct modeled after the Antarctic Treaty which designates the Arctic north of a selected parallel as a wilderness area.[17] Finally, a small subset of conservative congressmen introduced a 2009 bill proposing complete withdrawal from the United Nations, effectively ending U.S. participation in a wide variety of multilateral partnerships; the bill is under review in the House Foreign Affairs committee.[18] Strong opposition to partnership is balanced by those who have durable arguments in favor of this action.

In support of multilateral Arctic partnerships are a number of broad-based and disparate organizations and policies nonetheless unified in support of the issue; additional support comes from consequential benefits inherent in UNCLOS accession. Overarching is the National Security Presidential Directive 66 (NSPD-66) *Arctic Region Policy* released in 2009. Among the NSPD-66 policy statements is a robust admonishment for accession to UNCLOS:

> Joining [the UNCLOS treaty] will serve the *national security interests* … secure U.S. *sovereign rights* over extensive maritime areas … *promote U.S. interests* in the environmental health of the oceans … give the United States a *seat at the table when the rights that are vital to our interests are debated and interpreted* … [and] achieve *international recognition and legal certainty* for our extended continental shelf.[19] [emphasis added]

Furthermore, NSPD-66 persuasively promotes multinational partnership in the Arctic to address the myriad of issues faced in the region.[20] Likewise, the Department of Defense, as articulated in its 2010 *Quadrennial Defense Review*, strongly advocates accession to UNCLOS in order to support cooperative engagement."[21] Also among the tenacious supporters of accession are the U.S. Navy whose leadership stresses that UNCLOS *will protect* patrol rights in the Arctic and a number of environmental groups who want to advocate on behalf of Arctic fauna and flora.[22] In addition, the oil industry lobby representing Chevron, Exxon-Mobile, and Conoco-Phillips asserts that oil and gas exploration cannot reasonably occur without the legal stability afforded in UNCLOS.[23] In a consequential benefit of accession, United States' extended continental shelf claims could add 100,000 square miles of undersea territory in the Gulf of Mexico and on the east coast plus another 200,000 square miles in the Arctic.[24] Accession acts to strengthen and extend Arctic jurisdiction, open up additional hydrocarbon and mineral resource opportunities, add to the stability of the international Arctic framework, and boost the legal apparatus for curtailing maritime trafficking and piracy.[25] The benefits appear to outweigh the costs as the United States is increasingly moving to a position of strategic disadvantage in shaping Arctic region policy outcomes by failing to ratify UNCLOS.[26] This stands in stark contrast to other Arctic nations who have all acceded to UNCLOS and are moving swiftly to assert and consolidate interests in the region.

Analysis of Multinational Moves in the Arctic

Only when the ice breaks will you truly know who is your friend and who is your enemy.
-Inuit proverb

International state actors are far outpacing the United States in Arctic presence and preparedness for what the future of the region may hold. The so called –Arctic Five" nations of Canada, Denmark (via Greenland), Norway (via Svalbard), Russia, and the United States all have sovereign coastlines in the area.[27] The former four nations are making obvious Arctic inroads and in some cases aggressive programmatic initiatives in preparation for their exploitation of Arctic opportunities. The promise of vast, predominantly untapped resources and national security concerns are at the heart of these international moves. Infrastructure improvements, fleet expansion, increased military presence, and often conflicting territorial claims dominate the actions of the ―Arctic Five" in extending the protection of perceived national interests, sans the United States which ―has remained largely on the sidelines."[28]

In uncharacteristic political maneuvering, Canada has demonstrated significant strides in their Arctic preparedness and asserted their bold national Arctic policy through both rhetoric and action. In reference to claims of sovereignty in the region, Canadian Prime Minister Harper has frequently declared ―Use it or lose it," illustrating a new, almost nationalistic fervor that resonates well with the Canadian populous.[29] National impetus to support extended continental shelf claims and secure economic interests has resulted in the allocation of $109 million for Arctic seabed scientific research intended to be complete by 2014.[30] Similarly, Canada is expanding the existing deep-water docking port, a project dating to 2009, into a $100 million naval base on Baffin Island.[31] Additional allocations include a new $675 million ice breaker in 2010, establishment of a Canadian Forces winter fighting school in Resolute Bay near the Northwest Passage, and an initiative to build six to eight ice hardened offshore patrol vessels, the first of which will be delivered in 2014.[32] Presence and visibility in the Arctic have been bolstered by sponsorship of three major sovereignty exercises annually including the joint and combined Operation NANOOK.[33] Incorporating air, land, and maritime forces to demonstrate and exercise operational capability in the Arctic region, the purpose of these exercises is unequivocally ―designed to project Canadian sovereignty in the High Arctic."[34] Canada also maintains a staunch position on the sovereignty of the Northwest Passage as internal waters, a claim refuted by the United States who contends these waters are international straits.[35]

Similarly, Canada asserts overlapping territorial claims with the United States in the Beaufort Sea and the maritime border between Alaska and Yukon, with Russia in conflicting extended continental shelf claims, and with Denmark over Hans Island in the Nares Strait.[36] With its fleet of 12 existing icebreakers and programmed additions noted above, national-level emphasis on planning, preparedness, and presence, plus the legal basis granted as a signatory to UNCLOS, Canada appears well ahead of the United States in its ability to address vital national interests in the Arctic.[37]

Danish extensions into the realm of Arctic issues track along the major subject areas of sovereignty and security, economic interests, and political activism. Denmark's precarious tie as one of the ―Arctic Five" lies in Greenland, historically a colonial possession whose relationship to the parent Denmark has evolved into the present day status of self-rule. Under self-rule, Greenland is autonomous in many domestic respects but still supported by Denmark in the areas of ―defense, foreign policy, sovereignty control, and other authority tasks," providing the parent country broad powers to deal with Arctic issues.[38] Denmark shares competing claims to the hotly contested Lomonosov Ridge with both Canada and Russia, all of which believe the ridge is an extension of their continental shelves and rich in hydrocarbon reserves.[39] In an interesting dichotomy, Denmark and Canada are working together in a joint scientific venture to map their respective continental shelves despite the perceived encroachment by the Canadians into Danish claimed Hans Island waters.[40] In response to sovereignty concerns generated by Canadian and Russian moves and the general increase in Arctic activity, Danish military forces are adapting by reorganizing and combining their Greenland and Faroe Commands into a joint service Arctic Command and creating an Arctic Response Force.[41] While neither of these moves will increase the size of the Danish forces appreciably, it nonetheless demonstrates the emphasis Danes place on the region.[42] Force basing at both Thule Air Base in northwestern Greenland and Station Nord in extreme northeastern Greenland combined with $117 million in military upgrades in country, use of combat aircraft for surveillance and sovereignty missions, and an impressive maritime presence including RDN Vaedderen, one of a select few frigates in the world built to operate in Arctic ice conditions, demonstrate credible Danish resolve and capability to exercise presence in the region.[43] Economically, Greenland and surrounding waters promise a resource rich environment with 2008 estimates ranking the area as 19th out of 500 of the world's largest potential oil producing areas, plus receding ice is exposing potential mining areas rich in a number of minerals including large diamond reserves.[44] Leveraging both credible forces with potential economic boom, Danish international politics has improved their standing in the Arctic arena. Through leadership on the Arctic Council, organizing support for and brokering the Ilulissat Declaration, and assuming the lead for the Copenhagen Climate Change Summit, Denmark has attempted to become a more influential political player in addressing international Arctic issues and appears to be well on the road towards the ability to deal with vital national interests in the region.[45]

Norway has capitalized on a concerted national planning and preparation effort driving a number of key successful regional actions in preservation of its ―High North" interests. As the second nation to submit an extended continental shelf claim to the United Nations Commission on the Limits of the Continental Shelf, it was the first such claim to be recognized and approved.[46] This development, combined with skillful bilateral Russian engagement resulting in the resolution of a 40-year old border dispute in the Barents Sea, solidified in international law Norway's impressive Arctic maritime domain.[47] The country quickly put this success to work by opening up a new oil field in the western Barents Sea ahead of its Russian counterparts.[48]

Articulated in its *High North Strategy*, a whole-of-government approach characterizes the nation's resolve to ‑exercise our authority [in the Arctic] in a credible, consistent and predictable way."[49] With largely successful diplomatic efforts and an ongoing commitment to bilateral and multilateral cooperation, Norway has also strengthened military presence demonstrating a northward shift in strategic focus. A large portion of the armed forces, including its modern frigate fleet, jet fighter forces, and the army staff have been moved north with relocation of the joint headquarters inside the Arctic circle.[50] Oslo has also committed to buy 48 F-35 fighter aircraft and negotiated the addition of advanced air-to-sea missiles to the purchase.[51] This action clearly demonstrates the nation's stated objectives of enabling ‑Norway to exercise its sovereign authority and … maintain its role in resource management [in the High North]."[52] Norway's strategy also underscores programs necessary to further develop the capacity to safeguard Nordic interests; coordinated research programs are in force in both governmental and private sector institutions.[53] Anticipating the increase in maritime traffic through Norwegian exclusive economic zone waters and following an aggressive development program, Norway launched an experimental advanced technology satellite to provide high fidelity regional ship tracking.[54] The multifaceted and pragmatic approach to Arctic policy issues, combined with advanced planning, strong presence, diplomatic efforts, and rule of law in approved continental shelf extensions has Norway well positioned to exploit and capitalize on opportunities in the Arctic.

With the largest swath of Arctic territory in the world, state policy and action has garnered Russia the reputation of ‑the most determined and assertive player in the [region]."[55] Economic interests, infrastructure and transportation means, plus formidable military presence illustrate the advanced state of Russian preparedness for Arctic opportunities. Both major policy documents, the *National Security Strategy of the Russian Federation until 2020* (published May

2009) and *The Fundamentals of State Policy of the Russian Federation in the Arctic in the Period up to 2020 and Beyond* (adopted September 2008) strongly articulate the critical importance of the region as its —top strategic resource base."[56] This stance appears well-founded as one fifth of the country's gross domestic product and exports totaling 22 percent are generated in the Arctic. Similarly, estimates of up to 90 percent of Russia's oil and gas reserves are in the Arctic region; expansion, exploitation, and protection of these resources are deemed —crucially important for Russia's further wealth, social and economic development and competitiveness on global markets."[57] To gain access to these lucrative riches, Russia was the first to file an extended continental shelf claim in 2001. However, the United Nations Commission on the Limits of the Continental Shelf determined there was insufficient evidence to approve the claim.[58] As a result, an ambitious research effort is underway to complete geographical studies necessary to support the claim, including use of the Northern Fleet submarine forces. These efforts are to be complete sometime between 2011 and 2015.[59]

Moscow appears to perceive itself as the leading Arctic power with the most to gain, a perception supported by impressive plans and resources.[60] The country operates the largest icebreaker fleet in the world with 20 ships, seven of which are nuclear powered.[61] Nonetheless, many of these ships are reaching the end of their service lives resulting in significantly reduced ice breaking capability by 2020.[62] However, continued investment in new ice-breaking technology and partnership with the Russian private sector drove the deployment of new —double acting" tankers and cargo vessels. These vessels employ —azimuthal pod" propulsion with the ability to cruise bow-first in open water for good performance and stern-first in ice conditions using its reinforced ice-breaking aft hull. The newest such vessel was commissioned in 2010 bringing the fleet of the state-owned shipping company, Sovcomflot, up to three, each with a

70,000 ton capacity.[63] Additional capability, in the form of diesel-electric icebreakers is intended to replace that lost as the Soviet-era nuclear fleet ages.[64] Maritime fleet upgrades are interwoven with planned infrastructure support in the *Transport Strategy of the Russian Federation to 2030* which includes upgrade of existing Arctic ports and new development on both the Russian regional oceans and inland waterways.[65] Also key to the transportation strategy are the Northern Sea Route and Northeast Passage, a number of straits in and between the Russian Arctic archipelagos to which Moscow claims all as sovereign internal waters to be administered according to state regulations. Among these regulations is the requirement for all ships to provide advance notice of passage and apply for guidance through the route; implied here is also the payment of a fee for services rendered, a sea based toll-way of sorts.[66]

In defense and protection of the border and resource areas, Russia continues to bolster military presence and capability in the Arctic. In addition to the Northern Fleet whose naval military capabilities run the full gamut of surface and subsurface operations, Moscow created the Federal Security Service Coastal Boarder Guard.[67] Additional activities in the border and coastal areas include development of control infrastructure and equipment upgrades for the border guard, implementation of an integrated oceanic monitoring system for surface vessels, and a number of equipment and weapons testing and deployment initiatives.[68] Many of these initiatives demonstrate presence and resolve as in the 2007 launch of cruise missiles over the Arctic, additional Northern Fleet exercises in 2008, and the resumption of Arctic aerial and surface patrols not seen since the end of the Cold War.[69] While many of these actions may appear provocative in nature, Russia has also asserted commitment to working within the framework of international law, actively participated in the Arctic Council and other international bodies, and expressed interest and desire for partnership in the region particularly in the area of search and rescue.[70] In the aggregate, Russia emerges as among the most prepared of Arctic nations for the opportunities available and may well be poised to gain early regional commercial and military supremacy with the goal of similar successes in the international political arena.[71] Russian commitment to multilateral venues, along with the demonstrated attitudes of other Arctic nations, presents the opportunity for U.S. partnership in the region.

Opportunities for Partnership

Each of the ―Arctic Five‖ participates in a number of multilateral political venues and has expressed interest in partnership to address current and emerging regional issues. The Arctic Council, one such venue, was formed in 1996 as a high level membership forum to engender collaboration and cooperation on issues in the region; it has no legal authority through charter but has functioned well to promote multinational visibility and study on Arctic issues by all the Arctic states and indigenous peoples.[72] The 2009 report *Arctic Maritime Shipping Assessment*, a combined effort of a council working group from Canada, Finland, and the United States identified many areas ripe for cooperation including development of hydrographic data and charting, harmonization of regulatory shipping guidelines, and the critical lack of search and rescue (SAR) capability in the region.[73] Russia has taken the lead on SAR within the council for developing an international cooperation plan. With the Obama administration's intent to reset relations with Russia by seeking areas where the two nations can work together, SAR may prove to be a unifying construct mutually beneficial to all the Arctic nations, especially the United States.[74] Initial ground breaking work on the issue occurred in December 2009 in Washington, DC with additional discussions in Moscow the following February under an Arctic Council resolution to develop a SAR agreement; the archetype for a U.S.-Russian effort is coming into being.[75] Regional synchronization of SAR assets would address one of many U.S. critical capability shortfalls who has no Coast Guard bases on the northern coast of Alaska (the nearest of which is 1,000 miles to the south) and whose closest deep water port is in Dutch Harbor, over 800 miles south of the Arctic circle.[76] Another multilateral collaboration was the Danish-led Ilulissat Initiative which ultimately resulted in the unanimous Ilulissat Declaration. In the declaration, all the ―Arctic Five‖ nations affirmed

> … an extensive legal framework applies to the Arctic Ocean … notably, the law of the sea [UNCLOS] provides for important rights and obligations [and] *we remain committed to this legal framework* … [UNCLOS] provides a *solid foundation for responsible management by the five coastal states* and other users. We, therefore, see *no need* to develop a new comprehensive international legal scheme to govern the Arctic Ocean.[77] [emphasis added]

The significance of the declaration is paramount to cooperation in that UNCLOS provides the international ―common rallying point‖ for the Arctic states.[78] Similarly important, by virtue of the unanimous and strong affirmation toward UNCLOS, the declaration effectively delegitimized the notion to administer the Arctic along the lines of an Antarctic-like treaty preserving the notions of sovereignty and resource exploitation in the region.[79] With the United States' participation in these venues, and its support of UNCLOS publicly declared in both, failure to ratify the treaty suggests that U.S. credibility, legitimacy, and hence the ability to build cohesive multilateral partnerships is appreciably degraded. This conclusion is illustrated in Malaysia and Indonesia's refusal to join the Proliferation Security Initiative using the United States refusal to accede to UNCLOS as their main argument.[80] Accession to the treaty appears to be a key first step to preserving U.S. vital interests in the Arctic and building necessary credibility for regional and global partnerships in the political spectrum. Equally important to political partnerships in the region are those available through military collaboration of the Arctic nations.

There are a number of existing constructs for military partnership, most of which are currently bilateral and trilateral military-to-military ventures among the Arctic states and other interested states. The majority of these constructs are military exercises such as the joint Canadian-Danish-American ―Northern Deployment 2009" which promote interoperability and cooperation among participating nations.[81] Others include long standing mutual defense organizations such as the United States and Canadian integration in the North American Aerospace Defense Command, a standard which has been suggested for an overall Arctic collaboration model.[82] Similarly, the North Atlantic Treaty Organization (NATO) includes among its membership all Arctic states except Russia. While NATO supports member states and has exercised member militaries in the Arctic areas off Norway, it is a divisive influence when trying to include Russia in an Arctic solution set.[83] Ad hoc arrangements also promote cooperation as in the 2010 agreement between Norway and the United States solidifying a plan for the two national navies to train together in the northern Norwegian waters.[84] Another ad hoc relationship is also forming among the Scandinavian countries seeking to ―enhance security in the Arctic."[85] The North Atlantic and North Pacific Coast Guard Forums are multilateral organizations which promote information sharing and cooperative efforts in a number of maritime issues including search and rescue. These forums have been generally successful in promoting maritime cooperation through information sharing and interoperability through training exercises and may provide a model for similar cooperation in the Arctic region.[86] Another program which shows promise for a more broad based cooperative effort is the U.S. Coast Guard's ―Shiprider [*sic*]" initiative; under ―Shiprider" the United States and partner nations exchange maritime law enforcement officials on each other's patrol vessels allowing rule of law enforcement in both host and partner nation waters.[87] To one extent or another, all ―Arctic coastal states have indicated a willingness to establish and maintain a military presence in the high north."[88] However, decidedly lacking among the Arctic nations' military forces is a unifying construct to promote cooperation and mutual interests in an all-inclusive multilateral basis. This is similarly reflected in the U.S. military enterprise as there are currently no —mechanisms for joint operations in the Arctic."[89] Promoting a new broad-based military partnership paradigm to complement those opportunities available and emerging in the political arena seems to be the next logical step for preservation of the United States' vital Arctic interests.

The New Arctic Paradigm

Using SAR as the means to open the —partnership door," a non-threatening and apolitical issue of interest to all Arctic and other user nations, the United States, in coordination with Russia, should develop the Multinational Arctic Task Force (MNATF). Foundational support for development of the organization will be facilitated through a joint United States and Russia sponsored multinational SAR exercise involving all the Arctic nations, notionally entitled Operation ARCTIC LIGHT (OAL). Through the planning and execution of OAL, Arctic nations will build trust, exchange ideas, build relationships, and graphically see and experience the benefits of collaboration. The natural progression over time can be shaped toward formalizing the exercise into an overarching coordination organization which perpetuates OAL, along the lines of the North Atlantic and North Pacific Coast Guard Forums, which evolves into the desired MNATF construct. MNATF shall initially be comprised of the military representatives of the —Arctic Five" plus the additionally recognized Arctic nations of Iceland, Sweden, and Finland. The mandate of the organization would be the regional coordination, synchronization, and combination of member countries' SAR activities, resources, and capabilities to meet the needs of the region. The initial operational capability concept is a regional SAR organization that leverages the contributions of each member country into a synergistic operational command capable of responding rapidly to SAR crises in the Arctic region. Building on a model similar to the ―Shiprider‖ program, MNATF may expand mission sets commensurate with perceived regional needs and the desires of member nations to include rule of law enforcement on the high seas, resource protection, and anti-piracy/anti-terrorism. The outgrowth of this construct will be the improved safety, security, and stability of the region to the benefit of not only member nations, but the world at large. Corollary benefits of this new Arctic paradigm will include the partnerships formed and cooperation of nations through information sharing and capability integration. Finally, for the United States, MNATF effectively fills a critical capability gap adding credible action to the NSPD-66 *Arctic Region Policy* directives and supports the preservation of U.S. vital interests in the Arctic region.

Recommendations

Global climate change is a reality which offers opportunities in the Arctic for those nations prepared to capitalize on them. Many nations have moved forward with significant programmatic initiatives designed to extend sovereignty, expand resource and infrastructure bases, and build cooperative relationships in order to preserve and protect their perceived national interests in the region. The United States has lagged dangerously behind other nations in these preparations and is at a strategic crossroad if it wants to influence and shape the Arctic for its benefit. Vital to these preparations is for the United States to exercise a more active and leading role in Arctic policy shaping and to demonstrate credibility to act within the international legal system. To this end, the United States must:

1) Ratify and put into full force the UNCLOS Treaty. This is a key first step to provide the international legal baseline and credibility for further United States' actions in the region. While not *essential* to partnership, accession nonetheless demonstrates U.S. willingness to operate in a

cooperative vice unilateral manner within the international arena. Through UNCLOS, the United States will gain international recognition of exclusive rights over an additional 300,000 square miles of undersea territory along with the expected potential for lucrative hydrocarbon and mineral resources therein. Accession will also secure the United States a strong position to shape and influence the region for the preservation of its vital interests.

2) In collaboration with Russia, develop and execute the regional search and rescue exercise Operation ARCTIC LIGHT inclusive of all the Arctic nations. OAL will be a unifying catalyst among the Arctic nations promoting trust, cooperation, mutual understanding and will demonstrate the inherent benefits of capability synchronization in the region. The attendant organizational structure necessary to plan and propagate the exercise will provide the roadmap and foundational impetus for further regional partnership solidifying the gains hereto achieved.

3) Using SAR as the unifying point and building on existing multinational venues, lead the formalization of regional partnership into the Multinational Arctic Task Force. MNATF will be a cohesive and enduring organization that unites the Arctic nation's military forces and will complement political collaborations in the region. MNATF mission sets will expand from SAR to meet the emerging needs of safety and security at the northern most reaches of the planet. Ultimately, the United States in particular, and the world at large will benefit from a stable and secure Arctic region.

Conclusion

In conclusion, the United States must become more involved in the preparation for an ice-free Arctic and in the leadership of the region's issues. In this expansive geographic region, the issues are equally as expansive and require multilateral solutions to multinational problems. The recommendations mentioned herein are a foundational starting point for the United States to once again assert its historical leadership role during times of great change and in issues of great

importance. The opportunity is presented; will the Nation answer the call?

Notes

(All notes appear in shortened form. For full details, see the appropriate entry in the bibliography)

---

[1] O'Rourke, *Changes in the Arctic,* 6-7.
[2] Conley, *U.S. Strategic Interests in the Arctic*, 26.
[3] O'Rourke, 38.
[4] Conley, 2.
[5] *Circum-Arctic Resource Appraisal*, 1, 4.
[6] Nekhai, ―Russians Take Arctic Sea Route.‖
[7] Bacon, ―Ice Breaker,‖ 19.
[8] O'Rourke, 30-31.
[9] Thiessen, ―CG Admiral Asks for Arctic Resources.‖
[10] O'Rourke, 30-31.
[11] Comm. on Assess. of USCG Polar Icebreaker Roles and Future Needs, *Polar Icebreakers in a Changing World*, 1
[12] Ebinger, ―The Geopolitics of Arctic Melt,‖ 1220.
[13] Ibid.
[14] Morozov, *The Arctic: The Next "Hot Spot."*
[15] Borgerson, ―Arctic Meltdown,‖ 63.
[16] Ebinger, 1224.
[17] O'Rourke, 7.
[18] ―H.R. 1146.‖
[19] Crook, ―Comprehensive New Statement of U.S. Arctic Policy,‖ 345.
[20] Ibid., 345, 346, 348, 349.
[21] U.S. Department of Defense, *Quadrennial Defense Review Report*, 86.
[22] Demos, ―Arctic Circle Oil Rush,‖ 12.
[23] Ibid.
[24] King, ―U.S. Resistance to Sea Treaty Thaws,‖ A6.
[25] Ebinger, 1225.
[26] Conley, 26.
[27] Petersen, ―The Arctic as a New Arena,‖ 44.
[28] Borgerson, 63.
[29] Ibid.
[30] Conley, 17.
[31] Ibid., 18.
[32] Bacon, 18.
[33] Canadian Ministry of National Defence, ―Backgrounder,‖ 1-2.
[34] Conley, 18.
[35] Borgerson, 63.
[36] Conley, 16, 20.
[37] United Nations, *Chronological lists of ratifications.*
[38] Petersen, 38. Under self rule, Greenland has the option to become an independent nation, though to date has not exercised it.
[39] Ibid., 44.
[40] Ibid., 53.
[41] Danish Ministry of Defence, *Danish Defence Agreement 2010-2014*, 12.
[42] Ibid.
[43] Ibid., 12, 28; Huebert, *Welcome to a new era*, 1.
[44] Conley, 20; Peterson, 40; Ebinger, 1230.

[45] Peterson, 35; Conley, 20. The Ilulissat Initiative was a Danish led conference of the —Arctic 5" from which all countries unanimously affirmed that no additional international frameworks beyond the law of the sea were necessary in the Arctic effectively eliminating international proposals for a treaty modeled after the Antarctic Treaty of 1959.

[46] Ebinger, 1226; United Nations, *Commission on the Limits of the Continental Shelf.*

[47] Gibbs, —Russia and Norway Reach Accord."

[48] Ibid.

[49] Norwegian Ministry of Foreign Affairs, *The Norwegian Government's High North Strategy*, 7.

[50] Conley, 23.

[51] Huebert, 1.

[52] Norwegian Ministry of Foreign Affairs, 5.

[53] Ibid., 6, 23-34.

[54] —Norway's AIS satellite enhances marine safety."

[55] Conley, 24.

[56] Ibid.; Zysk, —Russia's Arctic Strategy," 103; Conley, 24.

[57] Zysk, —Russia's Arctic Strategy," 105; Zysk, —Commentary on Russia."

[58] Ebinger, 1226.

[59] Conley, 24; Zysk, —Russia's Arctic Strategy," 106. Completing the geographical studies necessary to support their claim is also articulated as a top national priority in the Russian National Security Strategy.

[60] Ibid, 103-104.

[61] Ebinger, 1220; Zysk, —Russia's Arctic Strategy," 106.

[62] Ibid.

[63] Antrim, —The Next Geographical Pivot," 25.

[64] Ibid.

[65] Ibid., 31.

[66] Zysk, —Russia's Arctic Strategy," 107.

[67] Antrim, 29.

[68] Ibid.

[69] Conley, 25.

[70] Ibid.; O'Rourke, 33.

[71] Conley, 25.

[72] Ebinger, 1226-1227.

[73] Arctic Council, *Arctic Maritime Shipping Assessment*, 5-6.

[74] O'Rourke, 32-33.

[75] U.S. Department of State, —Arctic Search and Rescue."

[76] Thiessen; Titley, —Arctic Security Considerations," 42. Distance calculated using straight line chart plot from Dutch Harbor, AK to the Arctic Circle boundary line at 66 degrees, 32 minutes north latitude.

[77] —The Ilulissat Declaration," 1-2.

[78] Petersen, 57.

[79] Ibid.

[80] King, A6.

[81] Conley, 11.

[82] Borgerson, 63.

[83] Anonymous, —NATO Parliamentary Assembly;" Byers, *Cold Peace.*

[84] Huebert, 1.

[85] Morozov.

[86] Canadian Coast Guard, —North Atlantic Coast Guard Forum;" Canadian Coast Guard, —North Pacific Coast Guard Forum: NPCGF – What Is It?" The North Atlantic Coast Guard Forum member countries include Belgium, Iceland, Portugal, Canada, Ireland, Russia, Denmark, Latvia, Spain, Estonia, Lithuania, Sweden, Finland, Netherlands, United Kingdom, France, Norway, United States, Germany, and Poland. The North Pacific Coast Guard Forum member countries are Canada, China, Japan, Korea, Russia, and the United States. Focus areas for both forums include maritime security, maritime domain awareness, search and rescue, illegal drug trafficking, illegal migration, fisheries enforcement, and combined operations. They are forums for dialog and coordination but have no legal or policy making powers. The cohesive nature of the forums promotes good relations and cooperation between the member nations' coast guard forces.

87 Attanasio, ―The U.S. Coast Guard Maritime Law Enforcement Academy," 68.
88 O'Rourke, 33.
89 Ibid., 38.

Bibliography

Anonymous. "NATO Parliamentary Assembly Discusses Alliance Role in High North." *Defense Daily International* 11, no. 9 (29 May 2009). http://www.defensedaily.com /publications/ddi/6965.html (accessed 16 Sept 2010).

Antrim, Caitlyn L. "The Next Geographical Pivot: The Russian Arctic in the Twenty-first Century." *Naval War College Review* 63, no. 3 (1 July 2010): 15-38.

Arctic Council. *Arctic Maritime Shipping Assessment, 2009 Report.* April 2009. http://arctic-council.org/filearchive/amsa2009report.pdf (accessed 13 September 2010).

———. "The Member States of the Arctic Council are: Canada, Denmark / Greenland / Faroe Islands, Finland, Iceland, Norway, Sweden, The Russian Federation and United States of America." http://www.arctic-council.org/ (accessed 14 Oct 2010).

Attanasio, Michael P. "The U.S. Coast Guard Maritime Law Enforcement Academy: Standardized training brings the U.S. Coast Guard closer to U.S. and international partners." *Proceedings of the Martime Safety and Security Council* 66, no. 1 (Spring 2009) 66-71.

Bacon, Lance M. "Ice Breaker." *Armed Forces Journal* 147 (March 2010): 16-19, 34-35.

Borgerson, Scott G.. "Arctic Meltdown :The Economic and Security Implications of Global Warming." *Foreign Affairs* 87, no. 2 (1 March 2008): 63.

———. "The Great Game Moves North." *Foreign Affairs*, 25 March 2009. http://www.foreignaffairs.com/articles/64905/scott-g-borgerson/the-great-game-moves-north (accessed 7 September 2010).

Byers, Michael. *Cold Peace: International Cooperation Takes Hold in the Arctic.* New York: Carnegie Council, 16 December, 2009. http://www.carnegiecouncil.org /resources/articles_papers_reports/0040.html (accessed 16 September 2010).

Canadian Coast Guard. "North Atlantic Coast Guard Forum." http://www.ccg-gcc.gc.ca/e0003559 (accessed 21 Oct 2010).

———. "North Pacific Coast Guard Forum: NPCGF – What Is It?" http://www.ccg-gcc.gc.ca/e0007869 (accessed 21 Oct 2010).

Canadian Ministry of National Defence. "Backgrounder: Operation NANOOK 10." July 29, 2010. http://www.canadacom.forces.gc.ca/spec/bg-nanook10-eng.pdf (accessed 29 September 2010).

Circum-Arctic Resource Appraisal: Estimates of Undiscovered Oil and Gas North of the Arctic Circle. USGS Fact Sheet 2008-3049. Denver, CO: U.S. Geological Survey, 2008. http://pubs.usgs.gov/fs/2008/3049/fs2008-3049.pdf (accessed 1 Oct 2010).

Committee on the Assessment of U.S. Coast Guard Polar Icebreaker Roles and Future Needs. *Polar Icebreakers in a Changing World: An Assessment of U.S. Needs.* Transportation Research Board Report. Washington, DC: National Academies Press, 2007.

Conley, Heather and Jamie Kraut. *U.S. Strategic Interests in the Arctic: An Assessment of Current Challenges and New Opportunities for Cooperation.* Report of the CSIS Europe Program. Washington, DC: Center for Strategic and International Studies, April 2010.

Crook, John R. "Comprehensive New Statement of U.S. Arctic Policy." *The American Journal of International Law* 103, no. 2 (1 April 2009): 342-349.

Danish Ministry of Defence. *Danish Defence Agreement 2010-2014.* Copenhagen, Denmark: Danish Ministry of Defence, 24 June 2009. http://www.fmn.dk/nyheder/Documents /20090716%20Samlede%20Forligstekst%202010-2014%20inkl%20bilag%20- %20english.pdf (accessed 30 September 2010).

Demos, Telis. "Arctic Circle Oil Rush." *Fortune* 156, no. 4, 20 August 2007, 11-12.

Ebinger, Charles K. and Evie Zambetakis. "The Geopolitics of Arctic Melt." *International Affairs* 85, no. 6, 2009, 1215-1232.

George, Jane. "The new Arctic policy: Canada chooses a buddy." *Nunatsiaq News,* 24 August 2010. http://www.nunatsiaqonline.ca/stories/article/2408103_ The_new_Arctic_policy_Canada_chooses_a_buddy_/ (accessed 2 September 2010).

Gibbs, Walter. "Russia and Norway Reach Accord on Barents Sea." *The New York Times*, 27 April 2010, http://www.nytimes.com/2010/04/28/world/europe/28norway.html (accessed 30 September 2010).

"H.R. 1146: American Sovereignty Restoration Act of 2009." *Govtrack.us*, 24 Feb 2009. http://www.govtrack.us/congress/bill.xpd?bill=h111-1146 (accessed 9 October 2010).

Huebert, Rob. *Welcome to a new era of Arctic Security.* Calgary, Canada: Canadian Defence & Foreign Affairs Institute, August 2010.

King, Neil Jr. "U.S. Resistance to Sea Treaty Thaws." *Wall Street Journal* 250, no. 44, 22 August 2007, A6.

Morozov, Yuri. *The Arctic: The Next "Hot Spot" of International Relations or a Region of Cooperaion?* New York: Carnegie Council, 16 December 2009. http://www.cceia.org /resources/articles_papers_reports/0039.html (accessed 18 September 2010).

Nekhai, Oleg. "Russians Take Arctic Sea Route," *Alaska Dispatch*, 20 August 2010. http://alaskadispatch.com/dispatches/arctic/6607-russians-take-arctic-sea-route (accessed 2 September 2010).

Norway's AIS satellite enhances marine safety." *Maritimejournal.com*, 22 July 2010. http://www.maritimejournal.com/features/onboard-systems/navigation-and-communication /norways-ais-satellite-enhances-marine-safety (accessed 1 October 2010).

Norwegian Ministry of Foreign Affairs. *The Norwegian Government's High North Strategy.* Oslo, Norway: Norwegian Ministry of Foreign Affairs, December 2006.

O'Rourke, Ronald. *Changes in the Arctic: Background and Issues for Congress.* Washington, DC: Congressional Research Service, 20 March 2010.

Petersen, Nikolaj. "The Arctic as a New Arena for Danish Foreign Policy: The Iluissat Initiative and its Implications." *Danish Foreign Policy Yearbook 2009*, 35-78.

"The Ilulissat Declaration." Declaration presented at the Arctic Ocean Conference Ilulissat, Greenland, May 2008. http://www.oceanlaw.org/downloads/arctic/Ilulissat_Declaration.pdf (accessed 22 Oct 2010).

Thiessen, Mark. "CG Admiral Asks for Arctic Resources." *Navy Times* (18 Oct 2010). http://www.navytimes.com/news/2010/10/ap-coast-guard-colvin-alaska-101810/ (accessed 19 Oct 2010).

Titley, David W. and Courtney C. St John. "Arctic Security Considerations and the U.S. Navy's Roadmap for the Arctic." *Naval War College Review* 63, no. 2, (1 April 2010): 35-48.

United Nations. *Chronological lists of ratifications of, accessions and successions to the Convention and the related Agreements as at 05 October 2010.* New York, NY: United Nations, 5 October 2010. http://www.un.org/Depts/los/reference_files /chronological_lists_of_ratifications.htm (accessed 7 October 2010).

———. *Commission on the Limits of the Continental Shelf (CLCS) Outer limits of the continental shelf beyond 200 nautical miles from the baselines: Submissions to the Commission: Submission by the Kingdom of Norway.* New York, NY: United Nations, 20 August 2009. http://www.un.org/Depts/los/clcs_new/submissions_files /submission_nor.htm (accessed 2 October 2010).

U.S. Department of Defense. *Quadrennial Defense Review Report.* Washington, DC: Department of Defense, February 2010.

U.S. Department of the Navy. *U.S. Navy Arctic Roadmap.* Washington, DC: Department of the Navy, October 2009.

U.S. Department of State. "Arctic Search and Rescue." http://www.state.gov/g/oes/ocns/opa/arc/c29382.htm (accessed 21 Oct 2010).

Zysk, Katarzyna. "Commentary on Russia: Arctic Strategy, September 2008." *Geopolitics in the High North*, 15 June 2009, http://www.geopoliticsnorth.org/index.php?option= com_content&view=article&id=2&Itemid=71&limitstart=3 (accessed 19 September 2010).

———. "Russia's Arctic Strategy Ambitions and Constraints." *Joint Forces Quarterly* 57, 2nd Quarter 2010, 103-110.